MY ALPHABET BOOK

This Book Belongs to:

____

Co-Author & Co-Illustrator

Aa

apple

Bb

baby

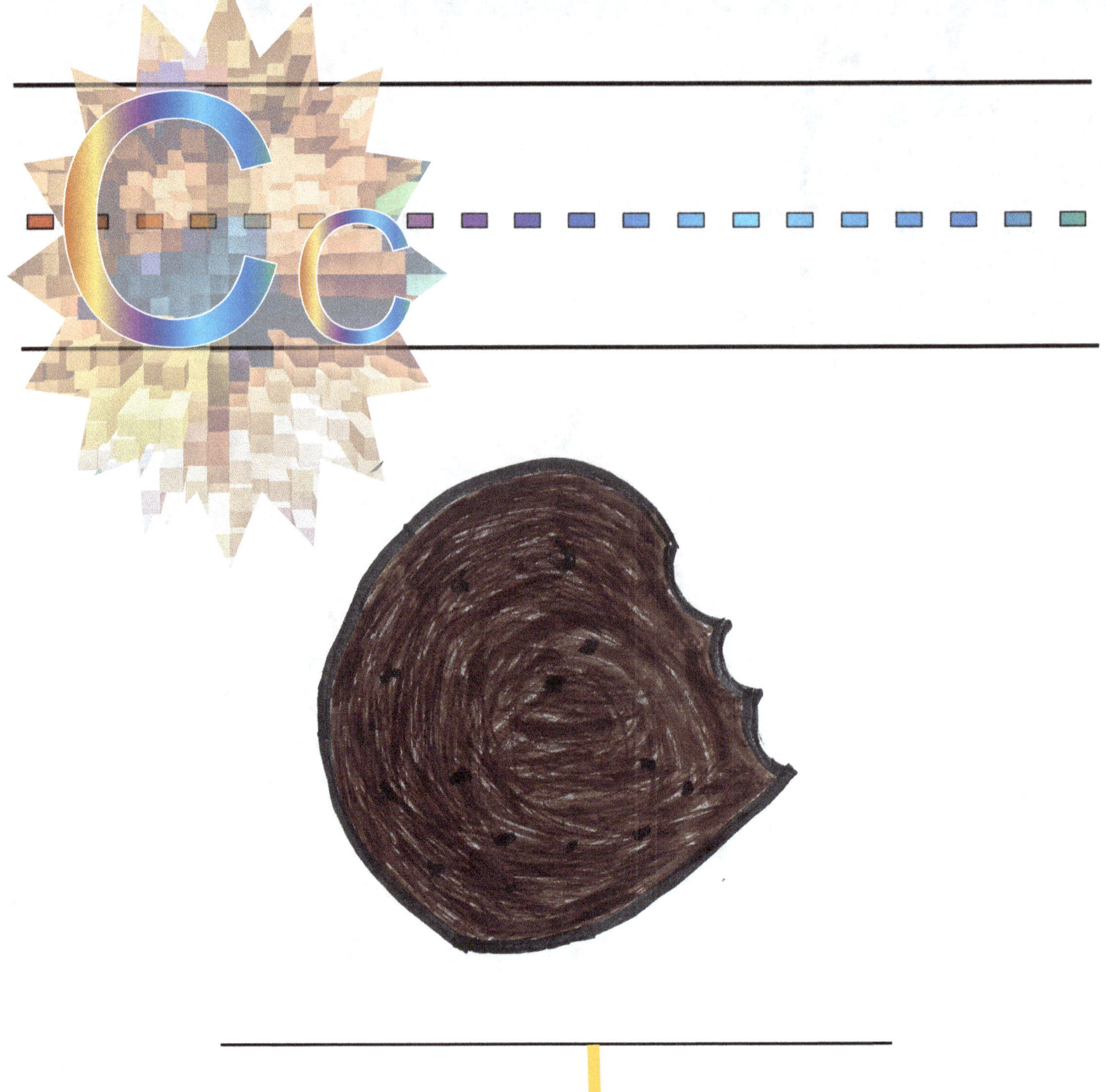

Cc
cookie

D d
dolly

E e

elbow

Ff

flower

Gg

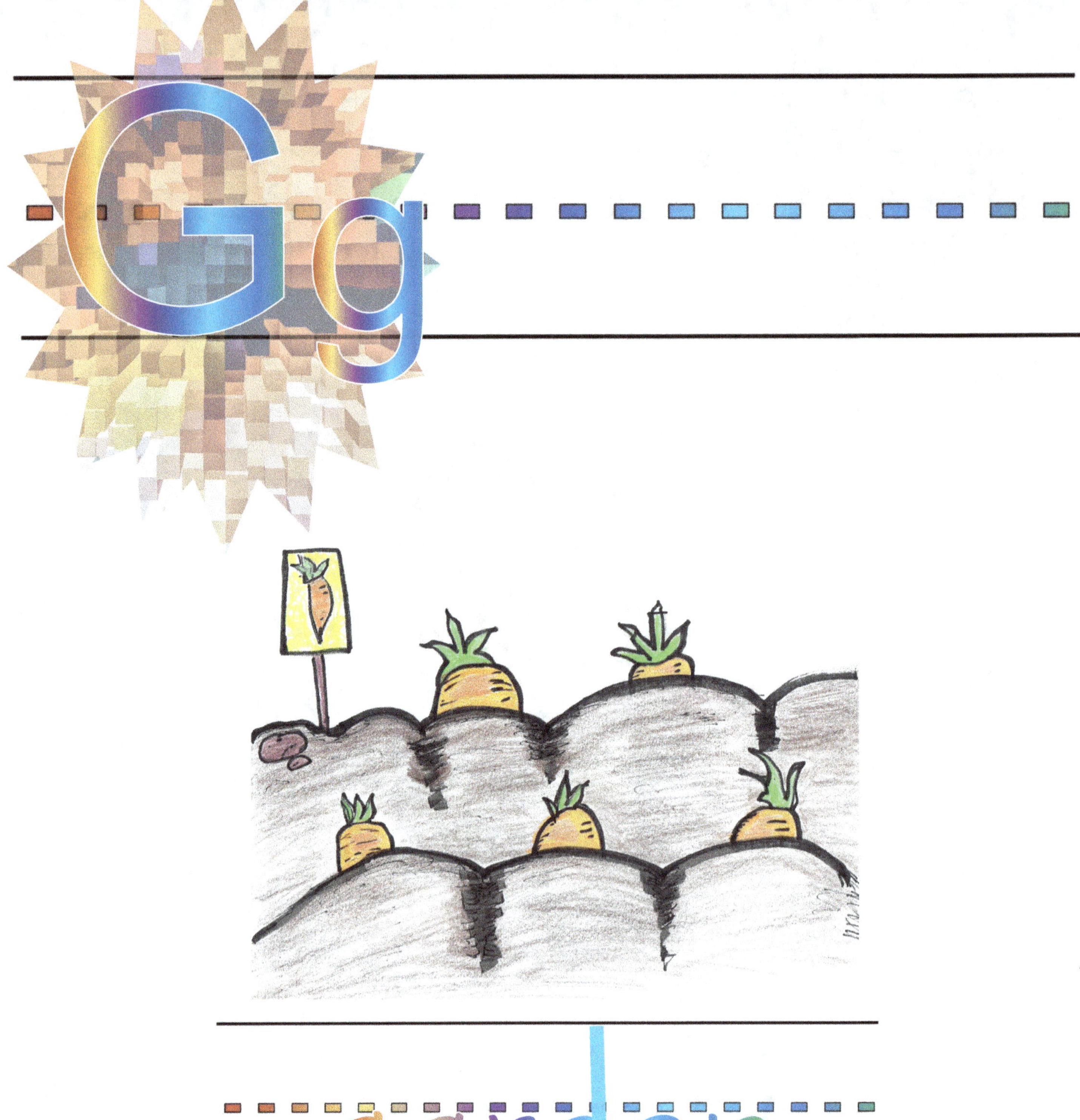

garden

Hh
hammer

igloo

J j

jelly

K k

L l
lion

Mm

monkey

necklace

Oo

ostrich

P p
pumpkin

Qq

quarter

rabbit

Ss

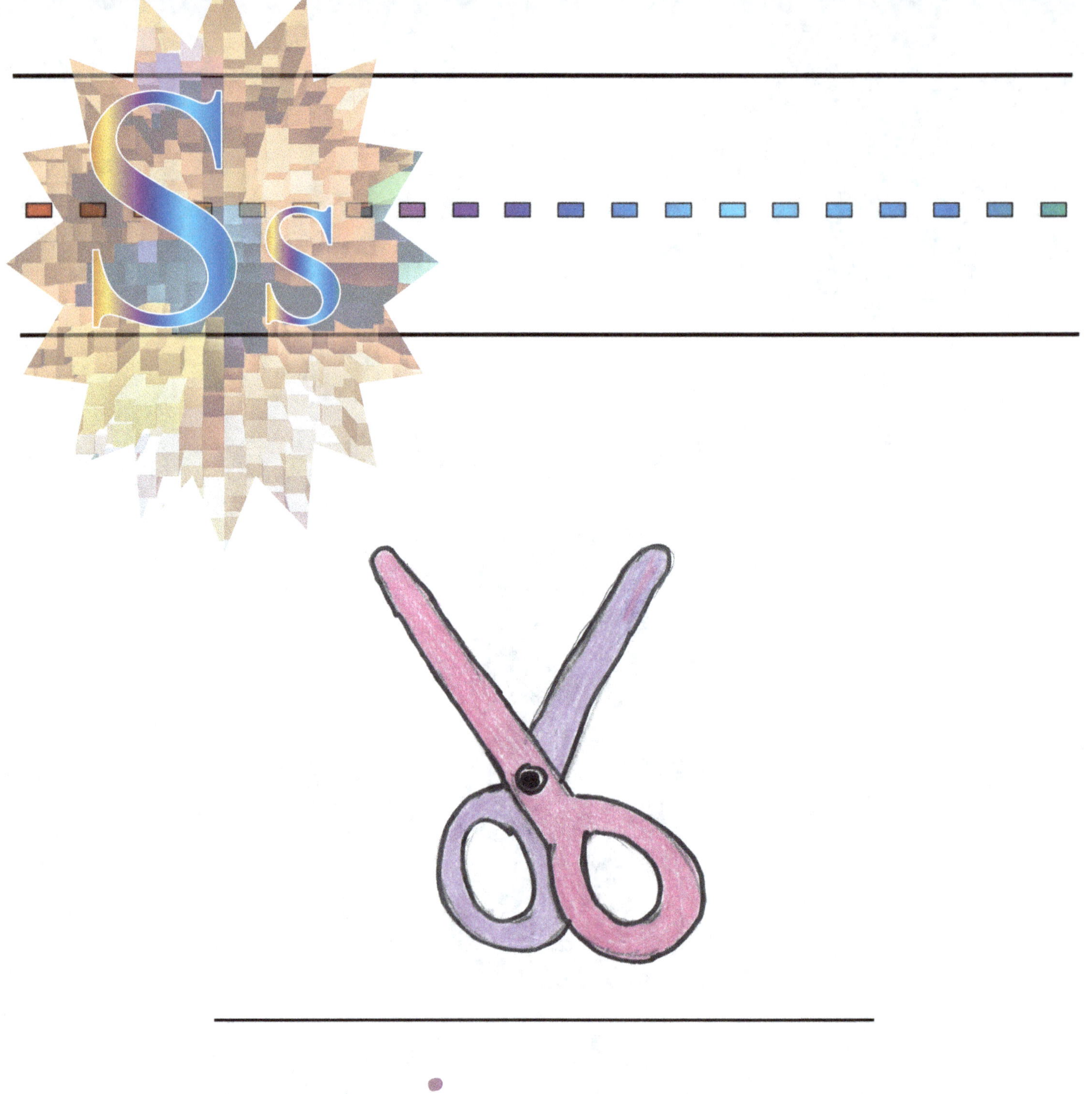

scissors

Tt
tiger

Uu

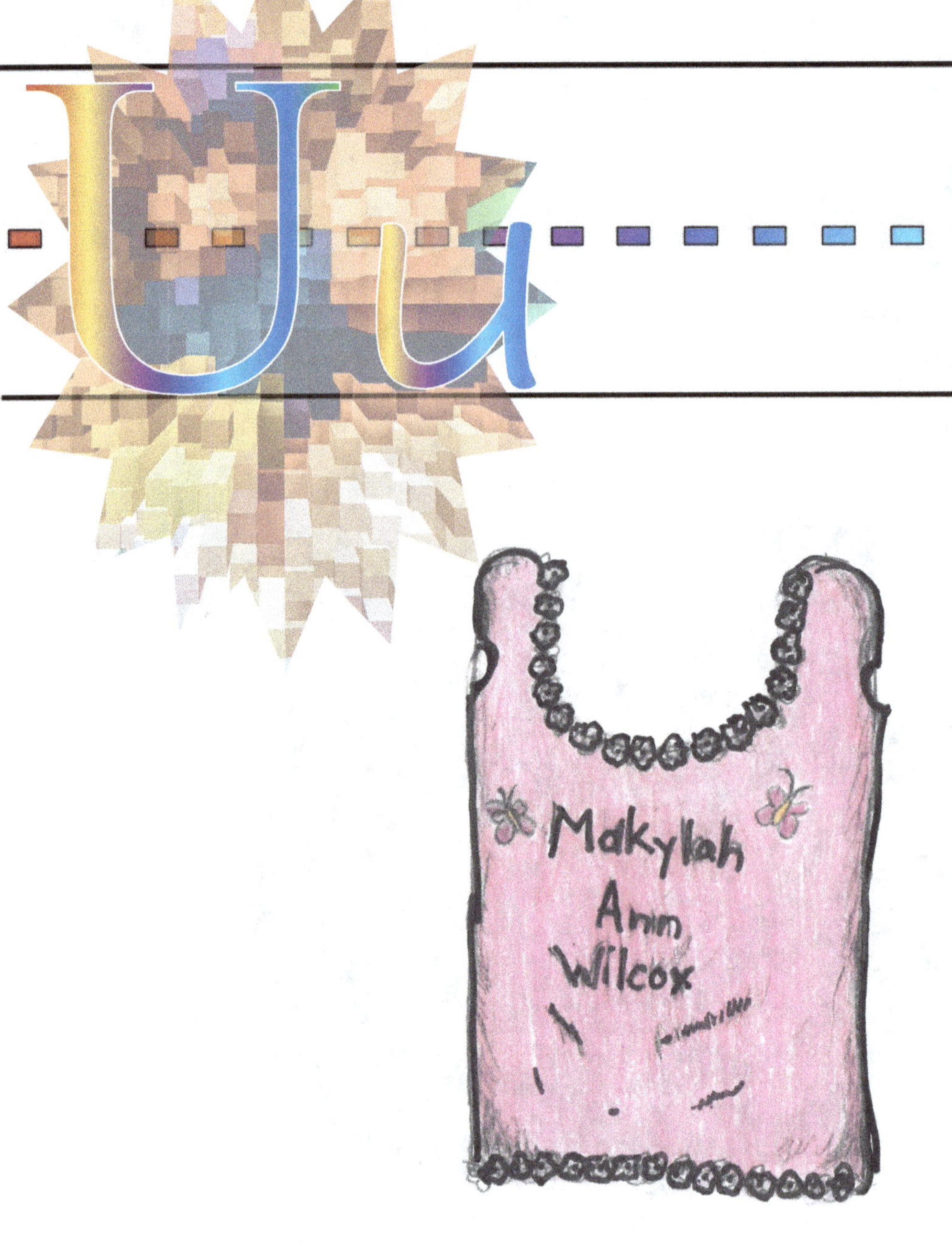

undershirt

Vv

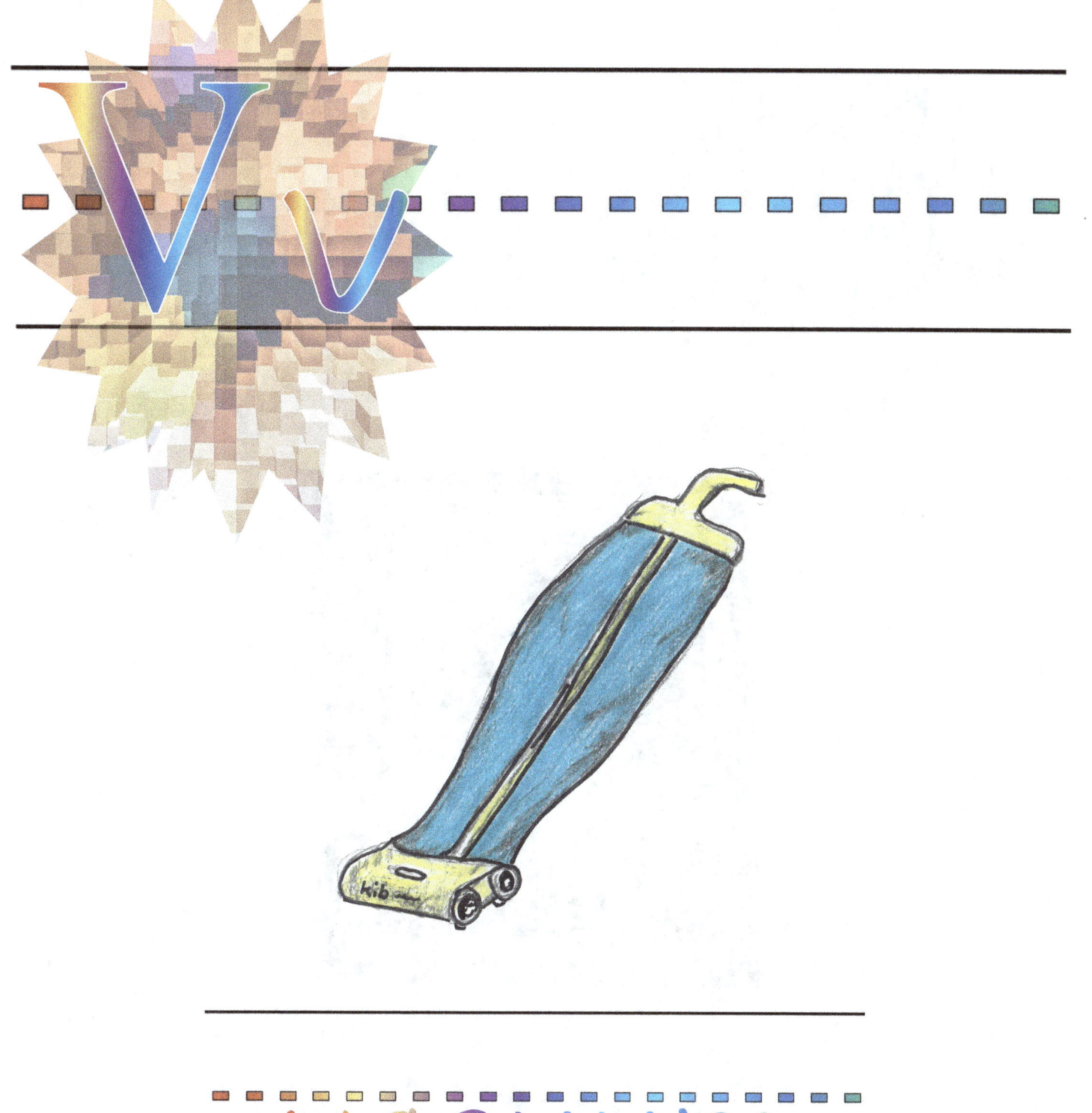

vacuum

Ww

window

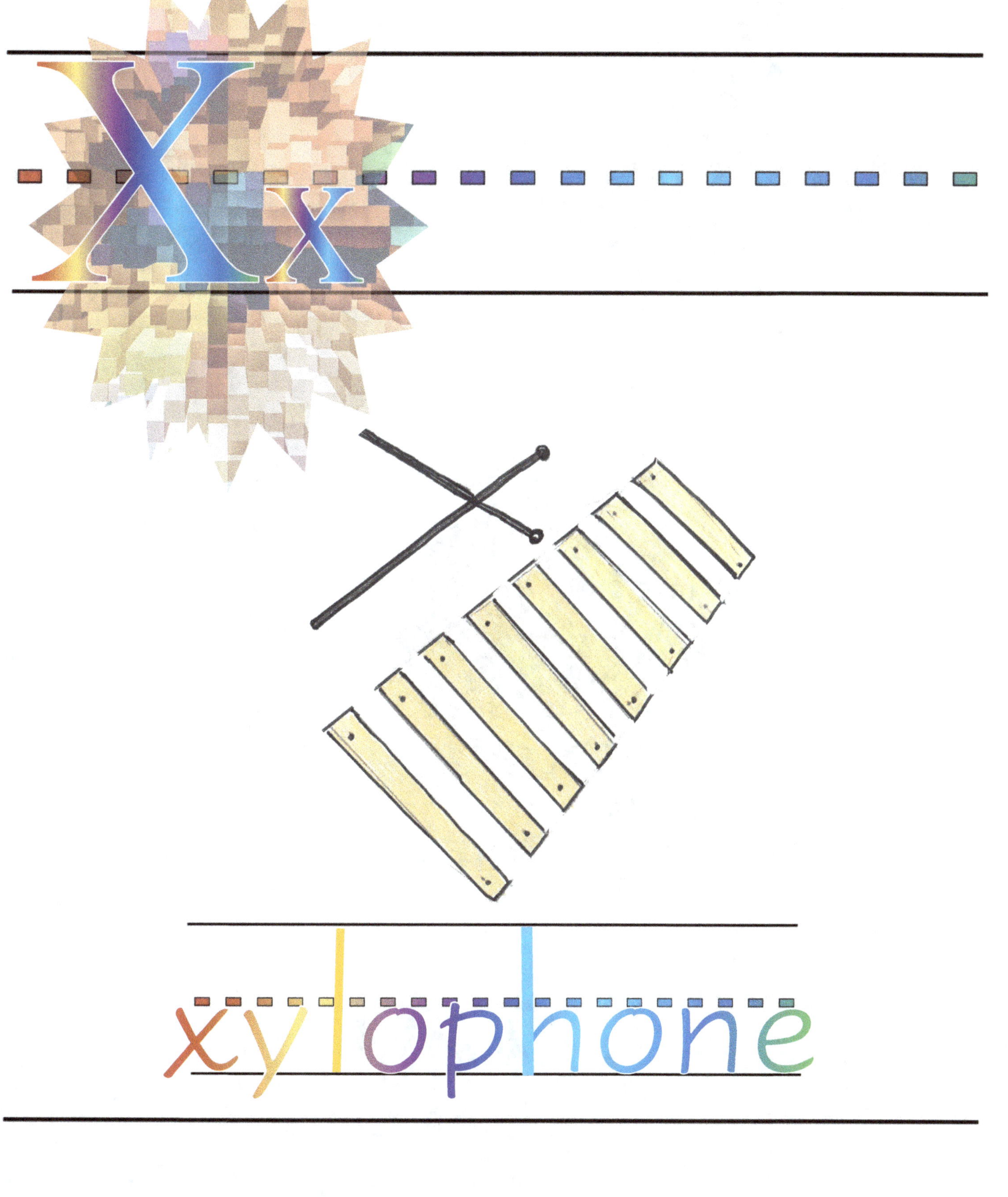

Xx
xylophone

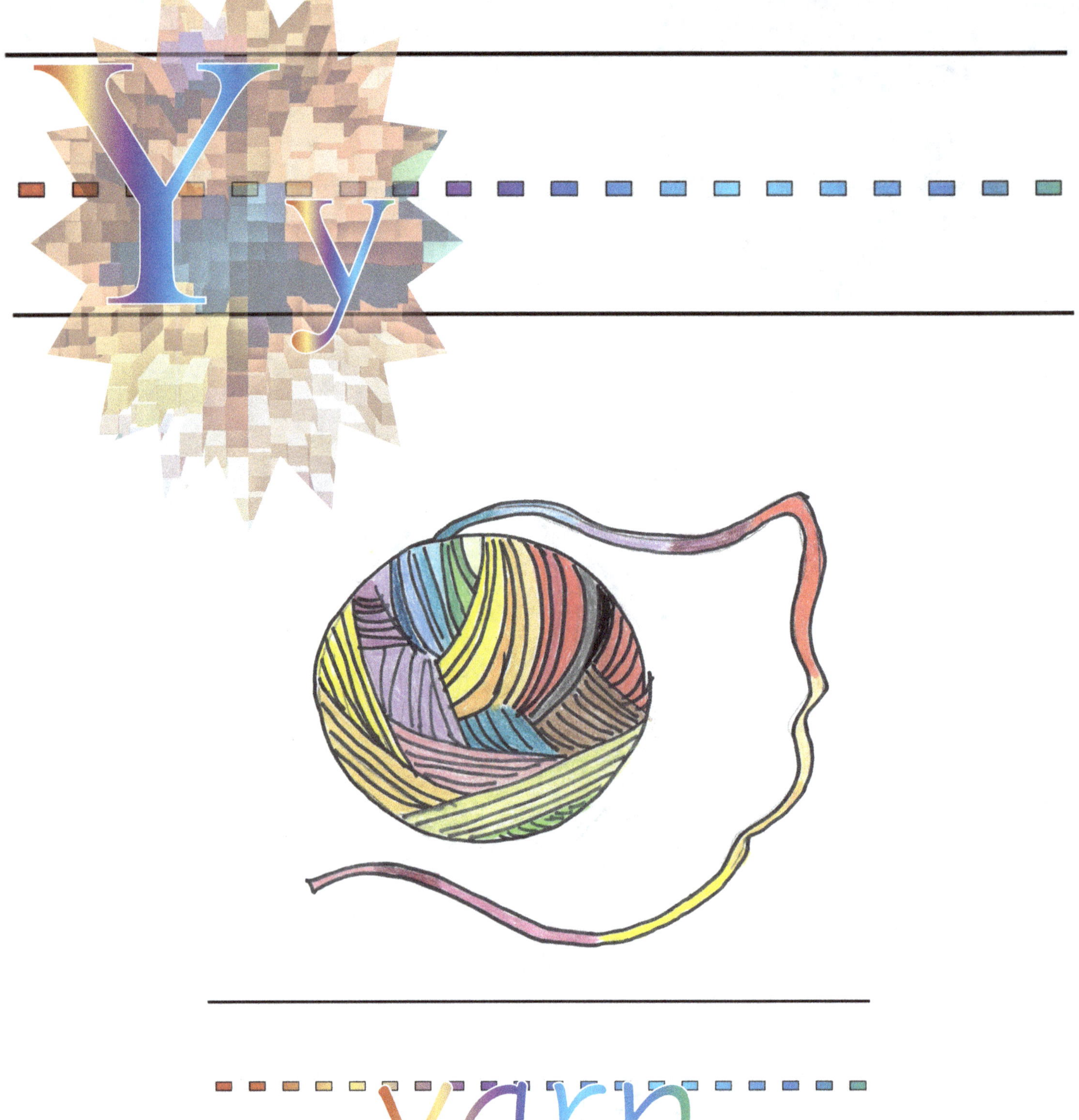

Y y

yarn

Zz

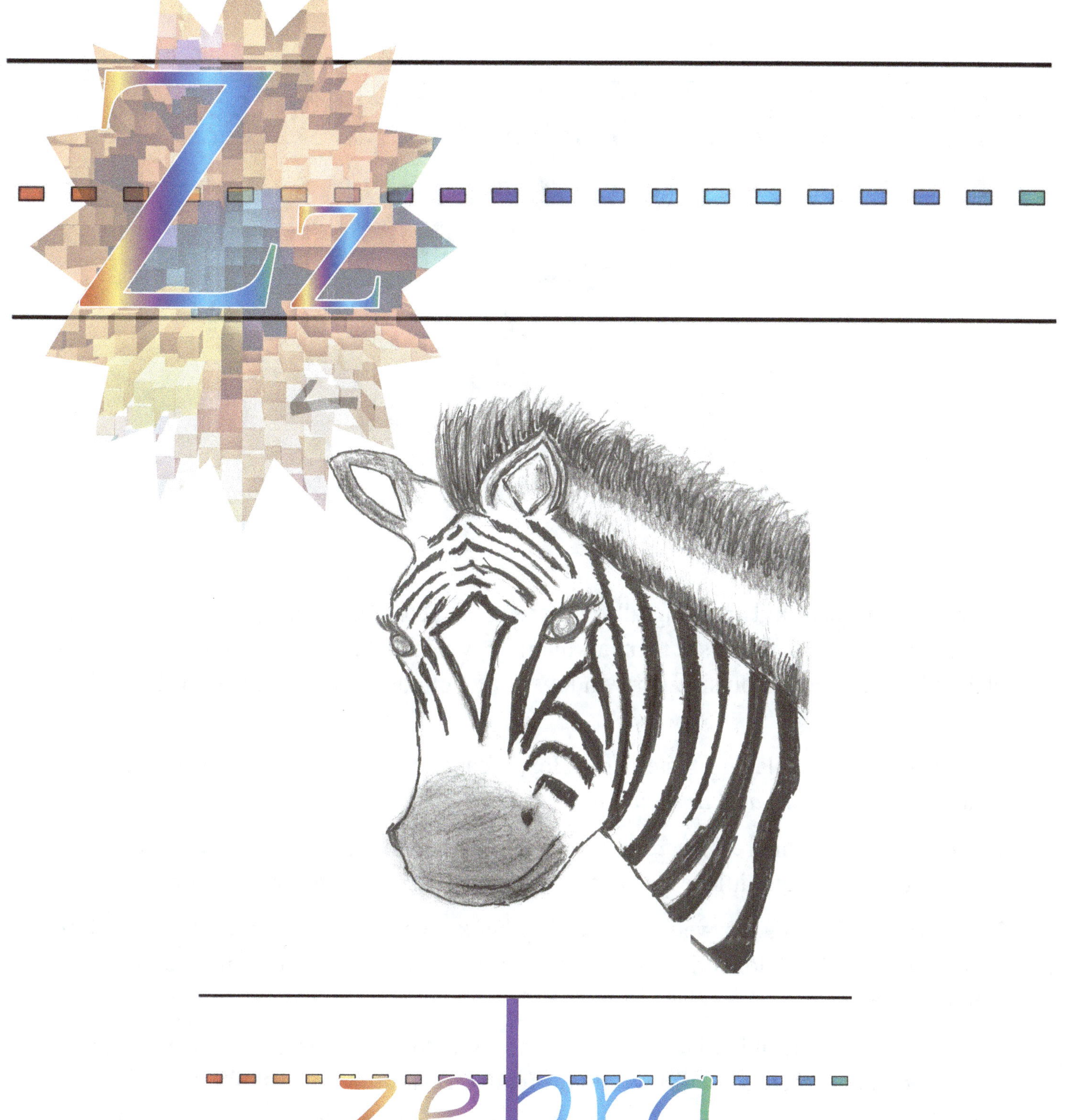

zebra

ABOUT THE AUTHOR

"Girl, look at them kids running all over the place acting like they got no sense at all. Lookin' like ragamuffins. I see them all the time, ya know? Humm," Sister Love Joy exclaimed as she looked outside her window at a commotion taking place in the parking lot.

In this scene, I am playing Sister Love Joy, a sassy Jamaican fireball, who walks like Mrs. Wiggins on the *Carol Burnett Show*.

I enjoy reading to children. *Reading Rainbow*, was one of me and my children's favorite shows when they were little, especially watching and listening to Lavar Burton.

I like art and drawing, as well as collecting books for myself and grandchildren. I am currently an early childhood educator at both my church and within my community - Cocoa, Florida.

I am a wife, mother, and grandmother. One of my favorite quotes is by Nelson Mandela, "Education is the most powerful weapon which you can use to change the world."

When I read to children, I like to make it dramatic and interesting. Seeing their responses inspired me to create my first children's book titled, *My Alphabet Book.*

Looking into the beautiful eyes of our children and grandchildren we think to ourselves, "This is my future, I am going to give them the best of me. I am looking at the future that is before me and they will do greater things with each passing generation."

-Colley A. Smith

2 Timothy 3:14-15

But you must continue in the things which you have learned and been assured of, knowing from whom you have learned *them,* and that from childhood you have known the Holy Scriptures, which are able to make you wise for salvation through faith which is in Christ Jesus.

Mission: To Proclaim Transformation and Truth

Publisher: Transformed Publishing, Cocoa, FL
Website: www.transformedpublishing.com
Email: transformedpublishing@gmail.com

ISBN: 978-1-953241-23-8